LAST
CALL

LAST
CALL

A Family's Battle with Alcoholism

S. HALE HUMPHREY-JONES, Ph.D.

Last Call

Copyright © 2024 by S. Hale Humphrey-Jones, Ph.D. All rights reserved.

No part of this publication may be reproduced, stored in a retrieval system or transmitted in any way by any means, electronic, mechanical, photocopy, recording or otherwise without the prior permission of the author except as provided by USA copyright law.

The opinions expressed by the author are not necessarily those of URLink Print and Media.

1603 Capitol Ave., Suite 310 Cheyenne, Wyoming USA 82001
1-888-980-6523 | admin@urlinkpublishing.com

URLink Print and Media is committed to excellence in the publishing industry.

Book design copyright © 2024 by URLink Print and Media. All rights reserved.

Published in the United States of America

Library of Congress Control Number: 2024912924
ISBN 978-1-68486-810-0 (Paperback)
ISBN 978-1-68486-811-7 (Digital)

12.06.24

DEDICATION

This book is dedicated to those courageous individuals, who have gazed into the abyss of addiction, overcame their terror, and began the long and treacherous course toward recovery. Also to the families who have struggled to create sense of their personal chaos to survive and continue to love and forgive.

You are the true heroes. God bless you all.

The more difficulty one has to encounter within and without, the more significant and the higher in inspiration his life will be.

—Horace Bushnell

CONTENTS

Introduction	11
Nine Lives	15
Love Hurts Too Much	18
I Want My Mommy Back	21
That First Drink	23
Other Choices	26
Oil And Water	27
Big Mistakes	29
Best Friend Forever	31
People Places And Things—Bad Influences	33
Down The Rabbit Hole	35
A Parent's Denial	37
A Parent's Worst Nightmare	40
Rehab	42
I Still Want My Mommy Back	45
Halfway House To Hell	47
Losing Hope	51
A Parent's Guilt	54
Saturday Night At The Emergency Room	57
You And Me Against The World	60
Antabuse—The Last Resort	63
Hitting Bottom	65
Alcoholics Anonymous	69
Freedom	72
Recovery	74
Coming Full Circle	77
Author's Note	79
Bibliography	83

INTRODUCTION

In researching *Last Call*, I was overwhelmed by the numerous and conflicting theories regarding alcoholism. In the *DSM-IV*, the *Diagnostic and Statistical Manual of Mental Disorders, Fourth Edition*, there is no disorder called alcoholism. Issues surrounding alcohol are categorized under either alcohol dependence or alcohol abuse. An individual is considered alcohol dependent if he or she develops a physical dependency on and tolerance for alcohol, such that it is difficult to impossible to go without alcohol for any period of time without withdrawal symptoms. Such individuals can be functional; they go to work, exercise, and appear healthy. But they drink daily. Others may not drink daily, but they become drunk, disruptive, or harmful when they drink.

Alcoholics Anonymous, which is the most commonly known approach to the treatment of alcohol addiction, identifies alcohol abuse or dependence as a disease. Individuals entering AA are expected to identify themselves as alcoholics. The belief is that alcoholism is a lifelong disease that has no cure, only recovery or remission from symptoms. The main objective of AA is complete abstinence.

Some individuals who have realized that they are abusing alcohol find that they can utilize a harm-reduction approach to control the damage. This approach involves limiting drinks, having a designated driver, only drinking at home, etc.

Harm reduction has been used successfully in drug addiction in such ways as providing clean needles and alternative medications to some drugs. The goal is to reduce the damage caused by the addiction.

Although total abstinence is always the ultimate goal, when it is not viable gambling-treatment providers often recommend harm reduction techniques. These techniques would include controlling the gambler's access to funds or limiting the use of credit cards and available cash while gambling. Sometimes educating the gambler regarding money management is helpful.

Harm-reduction techniques can also be utilized as a method of providing insight into the need for abstinence, as many addicts continue to believe they can control their addiction long after they have inflicted damage to their bodies, their families, and their lives in general. If these harm-reduction approaches do not work, if the individual continues to violate their own rules and boundaries, then abstinence may be their only option regardless of the specific addiction.

The biological (or genetic-enzyme) approach suggests that some of us are born with a genetic enzyme that will lead to complete loss of control overtime if the individual begins to drink. This theory states that during the early stages of alcoholism, the alcoholic appears to drink socially and that the drinking does not become identified as a problem until it is out of control. At this point, the alcoholic has difficulty accepting that they are not able to just drink socially. They make numerous attempts to control or hide their drinking, but continue to spiral toward devastation. For these individuals, there is no harm reduction.

Chris Prentiss, founder of Passages Malibu, does not agree with the disease model, or with the use of the term *alcoholic*. He states that individuals are not alcoholics, but they use alcohol—or other substances and behaviors—as a method of coping with unresolved issues or problems.

The one area of agreement among most theorists is that of abstinence. While some individuals who have overindulged in alcohol may be able to learn to drink responsibly, those who have lost control over alcohol should never drink again. Even a glass of wine or a beer can easily lead to a serious relapse. This makes a great deal of sense. If something has caused so much trouble in your life, why tempt fate?

Finally, it is clear that alcohol dependence or abuse does not limit its damage to the user alone. Over half of Americans say that addiction of some sort has had an impact on their lives. According to the National Institute on Drug Abuse (NIDA), $67 billion a year are lost due to substance-related crimes, treatment and medical costs, missed time from work, and social welfare programs. In 2006, there were 17,941 alcohol-related traffic fatalities. In 2004, substance abuse was the number one health problem in the country.

Alcohol is like a toxic wave that ripples all over the people who care or who are involved. Family members, loved ones, friends, community, colleagues, and society in general are all impacted by the damage created by this illness— whatever it may be called. Whether it is dependence, an addiction, or a disease, it is destructive to all who enter its wake.

Last Call was inspired by an actual family experience, although their names and specific circumstances have been modified for privacy reasons. There are many families just like this one. It is for these families and for those who love them that this book has been written.

NINE LIVES

They say that cats have nine lives since they are always getting themselves in impossible situations but somehow manage to survive. This must be true of drunks as well, because I know I should have been dead by now. I think this time, however, just might be my last life.

Why do radios manage to continue playing when the rest of the car is a mangled mess?

And why am I still breathing when this automobile is crumpled around me like a paper bag under a golfer's shoe? Yet here I am: heart and lungs somehow functioning, and nothing seems to be broken, or even bleeding. In a typical drunken-coping fashion, I crawled into what was left of my backseat and immediately went to sleep.

I don't know how long I was out, but the kaleidoscope of flashing lights penetrated my brain, forcing my eyes to flutter open—although they were far from focusing. The voice seemed far away. Was I in heaven? Oh, no, must be hell, hence the red pulsing flare. Yes, I was definitely in hell. Well, it was about time.

"Miss, miss. Are you okay? Do you require an ambulance? Can you move?"

Do people ask you questions in hell? Probably not. Damn! I think I'm still alive.

Somehow raising my head didn't take nearly the effort I expected, and soon I was able to climb out from the debris and stand in front of the very tall man in uniform.

"I think I'm okay," I responded in surprisingly sober fashion. Must have been out a long time. It was daylight, and I'm sure it had been dark when I hit that tree. What was that tree doing on the road anyway?

"We are going to have to get your car towed, but I think it's totaled."

I simply nodded. Yup. Not much to say to that. Car was gone.

"Perhaps you could take me to the nearest hotel. I can call a tow truck there and then get a rental car. I might want to rest before driving back home. I still have a five-hour drive."

"We can get the tow truck for you. I'll give you the number where they'll take it. Don't you think you should see a doctor?"

Why weren't they asking me to breathe into that thingamajig, or walk a line, or something? Didn't they realize how drunk I was?

"Uh, no, I'll get checked out when I get home, but now I just want to get a shower and call home, if that's okay. I'll call the insurance company at the hotel, and they can tell me what to I need to do." How was I able to talk to those cops like a normal person?

"Sure, if that's what you want, miss. Do you need assistance getting in the car?"

I just shook my head. I still couldn't get over the fact that they were being so nice and not throwing me in some drunk tank. Do they still have drunk tanks?

I got out of the patrol car, politely thanked the officer, took the information about the car, and dragged my duffel bag into the hotel. The clerk barely looked at me as he led me in, and I thought, again, that this luck just had to run out soon.

After a thirty-minute shower, I felt surprisingly good, although I began to think about getting a drink. That would have to wait. I had some calls to make. The toughest was to my husband. Perhaps this was where my luck would finally run out.

LOVE HURTS TOO MUCH

The sound of the phone ringing jolted him from his reverie. It was Shelly; he knew without looking at the caller ID. His emotions split him like a chopping blade. Yes, he wanted it to be her, wanted to know she was all right, and wanted her to be coming home—to him. Hearing her voice, he knew, would resurrect the intense pain he had been feeling for so long.

Shelly had been taking frequent trips to visit her friend Nancy. Cal knew she and Nancy would be drinking heavily every time. He Worried that she might not make it back from each trip. When she left this time he felt their marriage might be finally over. Now perhaps he could heal. The healing never really began, however. Would it ever?

For the past three weeks, Cal had carried her picture around, sobbing whenever Dani, his daughter, was out of earshot. He knew she could hear him moaning into his pillow at night, but he was unable to stifle the deep sadness that has become his constant companion.

How had so much joy turned so terribly bad? He missed his beautiful, happy wife, their laughter and their music. When did it go awry?

The first time he saw Michelle, he was emotionally cooked. She wasn't just beautiful—with her curly, golden-brown hair and warm, dark eyes—she was so alive. Her smile reached into his heart and gave it life. When he heard her sing, he knew that there would never be another woman for him.

Music was Cal's one outlet during graduate school. He loved folk music and played his guitar whenever he could get away from the boring business classes and books required for his accounting degree. The freedom of playing and singing was such a contrast with the seriousness of business school.

Their amateur band needed a female singer. Michelle was recommended by a friend, but didn't seem terribly interested. She finally agreed to sing with them one Sunday afternoon, but promised nothing. Her deep alto voice, in contrast with her lithe body, was a surprise to everyone. She gave a new sound to their music.

After a few Sunday afternoons, she agreed to become a regular part of their group. Cal watched her in awe for months before he got up the courage to ask her out. When she said okay, he was stunned. Two years later she agreed to marry him.

His hands were sweating so hard he dropped the ring three times. Then he started laughing nervously and couldn't get the words out. Shelly had to finish his agony. She just grinned at him and pulled him up.

"Caly, my caly, of course I will marry you. You are my best friend."

Cal was never sure what that meant, but it was good enough for him. He didn't even remember the ceremony, just that he was in complete bliss and remained that way for the first five years of their marriage.

When their daughter Danielle—they called her Dani—was born, he felt his life was complete. Shelly seemed thrilled to be a mom, and even quit her job to stay at home. They bought a big house when Cal graduated and got his first accounting job. Life was perfect—or so he thought.

The ringing continued. With a sign, Cal picked up the phone. Thank God Dani was with her grandmother. He didn't want her to see him fall apart.

"Shelly? Is that you? Are you okay?"

> Families are about love overcoming emotional torture.
> —Matt Groaning

I WANT MY MOMMY BACK

For the first five years of Danielle's life—everyone called her Dani—she was a happy little girl. She had two parents who adored her, and gave her hugs and kisses, and told her what a beautiful angel she was.

She never stayed with babysitters like other kids she knew. Mommy and Dad took her everywhere with them. They went to a lot of concerts outdoors where everyone played music and sang, and danced, and laughed. They drank a lot of stuff out of dark bottles and laughed even more. She sometimes fell asleep on a blanket and woke up in the car on the way home. She was happy.

She hated starting school; she wanted to stay home with Mommy and go places with her all day. Now she had to take a bus and couldn't go home until late in the afternoon. Dani believed that it was school that made Mommy sick. Mommy was never like that before she went to school, Dani was sure of that.

At first, Mommy just seemed very busy; she didn't seem to want to play with Dani as much and got angry with her a lot. Mommy never got angry with Dani before. And she didn't laugh as much as she used to.

Dani tried to get Mommy's attention and kept pulling on her while she was listening to a song. Mommy kept telling her to stop, but Dani wanted to talk.

Mommy slapped her across the face and yelled at her. Dani was so shocked she just stood still; she didn't even cry. Mommy had never hit her before or even yelled at her.

Mommy started to cry and grabbed Dani and held her close. "Oh, baby, I'm so sorry. I'll never do that again."

"It's okay, Mommy. I was bad. It was my fault."

But Mommy did hit her again, and yelled at her. Dani would to go straight to her room after school whenever she saw Mommy in one of her moods. Usually, she was drinking something purple, which she called her grape juice, in a big glass.

Daddy started looking sad too. At night, Dani could hear him cry, when he thought she was asleep. That was usually after Mommy yelled at him. She yelled at everybody now.

Dani wanted her old Mommy back, the happy Mommy who laughed and gave her hugs. She missed that Mommy a lot.

> Children begin by loving their parents. After a time, they judge them. Rarely, if ever, do they forgive them.
> —Oscar Wilde

THAT FIRST DRINK

My first experience with alcohol was when I was four years old. My parents had a big garden party. Since it was in the afternoon, and a lot of my relatives were present, I was allowed to stay up and attend. My mom was busy being a hostess, so I just wandered around from aunt, to uncle, and so forth.

People were drinking beer, wine, and drinks with umbrellas in big glasses. They would sit them down and walk away, forget where they were and go get a new drink. I was curious, so I began to sip from the one that looked interesting. Beer was warm and disgusting, and the wine tasted like medicine. But the drinks in the big glasses had lots of fruit and some foamy stuff that I really liked.

At first I felt good, but then I got really dizzy and needed to lie down. No one was really paying that much attention to what I was doing until I fell asleep under one of the tables.

Mom found me and decided I needed to go to bed. It wasn't until she picked me up that she smelled the alcohol and realized what I had been doing. I don't really remember what happened next, but I've heard the story told so often enough to repeat it.

The party ended abruptly. Morn was angry with everyone for allowing me to sip from the drinks, but most of all, she was mad at herself. What kind of mother was she? How could she have allowed this to happen to her own daughter?

As I've heard, I slept fitfully that night, yelling about pretty drinks and umbrellas. After that, I was always in bed during parties or with a sitter.

My next experience with alcohol was when I was twelve. It was not a good one.

I had just moved to a new school since my parents bought a house in another district. It was supposed to be a better school, but I couldn't seem to fit in with the other girls my age. I decided to get their attention by doing something daring. It turned out to be one of the stupidest things I have ever done.

Going into the liquor cabinet, I poured a little of various liquors into a glass jar. I took just enough so they wouldn't notice. Then I put it in my backpack and brought it to school. During the lunch break, I announced that I had a special surprise. Curious, the girls went out to the end of the schoolyard with me, and I brought out my jar of liquor.

The girls each took a sip, but then dared me to drink the rest myself. Desperate to impress them, and not realizing they were laughing at me the entire time, I choked down the remains of the mixture. Stupid? Oh, yeah!

The girls went back to class, leaving me to weave my way back to the building before I threw up in the hallway. Someone must have called the nurse because the next thing I knew, I was lying on a cot, and my mother was standing over me, holding my hand and asking a million questions.

Since no one was really sure how much I drank or what—the girls weren't talking—they took me to the ER, where they pumped my stomach and kept me for hours for observation. This was the longest afternoon of my life. When I woke up, I could hear my mother crying and talking to me, but I kept my eyes tightly closed. I wanted to disappear and never have to look at her again. How could I ever explain why I did something so dumb?

> Even a minor event in the life of a child
> is an event of that child's world and thus
> a world event.
> –Gaston Bachelard

OTHER CHOICES

Needless to say, I was not interested in any form of alcohol for a long, long time. When I began my foray into recreational substances, alcohol was not my drug of choice. My preference was pot. It seemed to be everywhere when I entered high school. Kids smoked it at home in the bathroom, and my parents had no clue.

It was funny because we had these major discussions about smoking cigarettes. My mom was totally sanctimonious about smoking and threw a fit when she caught me with a pack in my purse (unfortunately, I dropped the purse, and the cigarette fell out). Yet they never knew about the pot until I was in college, and it seemed like something all college kids did.

Beer had never been part of my early experiences with alcohol and did not have the same level of negative association. So it was not a difficult decision to begin adding a beer or two to my joint during the frequent keg parties. I found that a few beers would mellow m e out, but not push me over the line. I was often the designated driver. A lot of my friends would get drunk, sick, pass out, or get really hostile, but I was okay most of the time. Alcohol was not a problem for me—yet.

OIL AND WATER

I should never have married Cal. The truth was that I probably should never have married anyone. All of my relationships seemed to go south the minute a guy tried to tell me what to do. I liked my freedom.

Before I met Cal, I had been involved with a guy who seemed great in the beginning but then became jealous and suspicious. He wanted to know where I was all the time. I had a lot of friends and hung out after work, often coming home late. He began accusing me of seeing another guy so he wanted me to stay home more often.

One night, I came home late, and he was waiting for me. He started yelling and calling me *whore* and *slut*. I made the mistake of yelling back, so he grabbed my arm and threw me across the room. The next few minutes were a blur, but I managed to grab my keys and run to the car. I had left my pocketbook, my Mom always told me to keep money and an extra set of keys in the car for emergencies. I seldom listened to her, but thank God this time I had.

Two days later, my mom, some friend, and I moved my stuff into another place. He called constantly for about a week, but I never took his calls, and I never saw him again. After that, I was edgy when it came to men. Too much hassle.

Call and I knew each other from an amateur music group. I sang, and he played guitar. I knew he liked me because he always turned red whenever we spoke, but I never thought of him that way. Cal was just Cal, a nice guy.

The first time he asked me out, I thought it was just a group thing, but it turned out that it was just the two of us. I don't know why it progressed because he was never my type physically, but he was just so darned nice. I really like the way he treated me, like I was so special. I was waiting for him to get possessive or jealous, but he never did. I could do no wrong. He just wanted to be around me.

All my friends were pairing off. They were either getting married and having kids, or moving in together. I began to feel like a third wheel.

My mom, who had been divorced for years, finally remarried. My new stepdad was a real jerk. He kept pontificating about everything. I think my mom was impressed with this intelligence, but I thought he was a joke. He seemed insulting to both of us, so I didn't see her as much.

My dad had remarried right after the divorce, and his wife clearly was not interested in a grown daughter. I was feeling disconnected and left out. Perhaps if things had been different, I might not have said yes when Cal asked me to marry him; but he was just so sweet, and I wanted to be loved. Mostly, I just wanted to belong somewhere.

> The love that last the longest is the love that is never returned.
> —W. Somerset Maugham

BIG MISTAKES

I got pregnant with Dani the very month Cal graduated. He was over the moon with joy. I wasn't sure I would make a good parent, but I quickly got caught up in the excitement.

The first time I saw Dani, I felt an inexplicable combination of total love and extreme fear. She was so beautiful and tiny. My heart seemed to explode with love each time I looked at her, but what if I couldn't take care of her? What is I was a bad mother?

My job was a cable television producer had always been the love of my life. Now the thought of returning to work was unacceptable. My baby needed me at home. I never dreamed I would be that kind of mother. I always laughed at women who showed pictures of their kids and talked about toilet training. Nevertheless, my life seemed to be totally absorbed in my daughter.

As much as I loved Dani, not working or going to school was alien to me. I had this huge gap in my time. After reading the paper and caring for Dani, I would find myself wandering the house, looking for something to occupy my time. I became obsessed with keeping everything neat, unraveling if things became disordered.

Cal didn't seem to understand my need for neatness; he would laugh at me and tell me to "lighten up." He was always a bit of a slob, which I'd never realized before. He would drop his clothes on the floor and leave dishes all over the house. I spent each morning cleaning up after the mess he's made the night before.

I seemed to be responsible for everything at home—making medical appointments, meals, the whole thing. When I worked, we would get takeout a lot and never really worried about cleaning the house. We were completely focused on having fun and enjoying life. Now I was becoming a different person entirely, always irritated about something.

My one joy was playing with Dani. She was such a happy baby. We took her everywhere with us, never leaving her with sitters. Who could trust a sitter? Also. I nursed her until she almost a year old.

Nursing was a surprising experience. When she nursed, we were together in a world of peace and joy. I never knew parenting could be so exhilarating.

When Dani turned four, everyone insisted she go to preschool. I resisted, but finally caved. She needed socialization, I accepted that. That first day was agony leaving her in a room full of strange children and adults. I was certain she would be traumatized, but she seemed to love it. That was when I met Nancy (Nance), my bet friend and worst enemy.

BEST FRIEND FOREVER

Nancy and I sat outside the preschool for nearly an hour that first day, both hesitant to leave our precious offspring. Finally, we decided to go for coffee and talked nonstop for the next two hours. We were soul mates, both feeling displaced after quitting our jobs, both interested in music, politics, and sports.

We began picking the kids up together and going shopping, to the park, the carnivals. We were both football fans, and we watched games together while our kids played. It was during those games that the drinking began.

Cal and I often drank beer when we played music, but while I was pregnant with Dani, and while I was nursing, I didn't drink at all. As soon as the nursing ended, though, I began drinking beer with a vengeance. I realized that I had resented the fact that Cal was able to drink during my pregnancy but I could not. It became one more irritation.

At first, I found that drinking mellowed me out so that I wasn't so annoyed with Cal, but after a few beers, my irritation became fueled and seemed to explode. I didn't connect the drinking with the anger, however. It was Cal who was the problem, not the drinking.

Some of the guys in our music group began joking about my beer belly, asking if I was expecting again. Because I had been slim all my life, these jokes were a blow to my ego.

During one of my talks with Nance, I shared my concern about the beer. She understood completely. We were both into physical fitness, and even joined a gym together. It seemed a perfect friendship.

Nancy had the perfect solution to my problem. She introduced me to cranberry juice and vodka. After our workouts, we would get juice in the health bar. Nancy was big on cranberry juice; she said it cleaned you out. She also carried a flask of vodka with her in her tote bag. Just something to celebrate the workout, she said. Vodka and cranberry juice was a health drink and didn't give you a beer belly. It tasted good and quickly became my drink of choice.

Some people drink occasionally at happy hour, celebrations, or parties. Nancy and I drank all the time. It wasn't drinking, we rationalized—it was our health pick-me-up. I never thought of either of us as alcoholics. We were concerned mothers, and she was my best friend. We were happy, our kids were happy. Life was good!

> As long as you derive inner help and comfort from anything, keep it.
> —Mahatma Gandhi

PEOPLE PLACES AND THINGS—BAD INFLUENCES

Nance and I both complained about our husbands when we were together. We would grumble about their lack of involvement in household chores, or their insensitivity to our feelings. I didn't realize, however, how bad things were for Nance at home until she announced she was getting a divorce and moving away.

This was a complete shock. How would I function without her? She had become my escape from everything I had been trying to ignore about my life. The times we spent together allowed me to cope with the dirty dishes, and laundry, and my annoyance toward Cal.

Without Nance, I saw my life in technicolored clarity. I had been unhappy with Cal for a long time, and I hated not working. Dani was in school now, and I had nothing but housework and chores to fill my days. Getting back into my job seemed impossible after the long hiatus.

The drinking began as soon as Dani boarded the bus for school. At that time, I didn't realize that with each drink, I was chasing the joy I'd felt when the drinking first began in earnest. I was chasing my high, my escape. Unfortunately, there never seemed to be enough alcohol to reach that point.

I stopped going to the gym; it wasn't as much fun without Nance. Out of sheer boredom in the afternoon, I would go to a nearby sports bar, drink, shoot pool, or watch sports until it was time for Dani to come home. A couple of times, I lost track of time and would find Dani crying on the porch.

I felt guilty about how I was neglecting Dani, but mostly, I was just angry—angry at Cal, Dani, and my life in general. I lashed out at everyone, sometimes even hitting Dani, which was something I never dreamed I would do.

I made a friend, Cathy, at the sports bar, and we hung out a lot. She wasn't Nance, though, and I really didn't like her that much, but she also had a son Dani's age, and they could play together in the afternoon while we drank. The more we drank, the more we neglected our kids. They ran around without supervision . God must have been watching them because they never got hurt or worse.

I called Nance almost every day. She was depressed and lonely as well, and we talked for a long time. She kept asking me to come out to visit her. It was a long drive, but I needed to see my friend.

> If you're going through hell, keep going.
> —Winston Churchill

DOWN THE RABBIT HOLE

After a lot of whining on my part, Cal agreed to stay with Dani for the weekend while I went to visit Nance. I knew I couldn't drink while driving, so I kept the vodka in the trunk of the car. By the time I arrived, though, I was shaking so bad I could barely get the vodka out. I didn't even bother with the cranberry juice. Pulling the bottle from my bag, I gulped greedily until the shaking stopped. It had been a long while since I had gone more than an hour or two without a drink.

Nance and I cranked out the drinks and spent the entire weekend on the couch talking and drinking until we both passed out. It was a great weekend! I hated to leave.

Remembering the earlier drive, I allowed myself one large cranberry and vodka for the drive home. I figured that if I got stopped, I could just say it was juice.

After that, I made the trip at least one weekend a month. Each time, the drinking was heavier and heavier. Nance had even started taking prescription pills, Percocets and oxys. She said she got them for her back, but the pills and the booze made her nasty. She cursed and yelled about everything. The trips were not as much fun anymore.

The last trip convinced me that I might just have a problem. Usually, I would try to drive back in the morning, so I was somewhat sober. This time, however, I stayed through the day. By the time I left late in the evening, I was so drunk I don't remember driving until I woke up with the police lights in my eyes.

A PARENT'S DENIAL

The ringing of the phone at 4:00 a. m. was like a fire alarm. Calls at that hour could never be good news. Jessica's first thought was that something happened to her daughter, Shelley, or her granddaughter, Dani. A car accident? Fire? She stumbled to the phone in panic. "Hello, hello."

"Mrs. Collins, this is Nancy, Shelley's friend."

"Yes, Nance, what's wrong? Have you moved back to the area?"

"No, Shelley was visiting me. She went back home yesterday. We had a big fight, but that's not why I'm calling you. Mrs. Collins, I think Shelley's in trouble."

"What? A car accident? Is she alive? Oh, God, please let her be alive."

"No, no, nothing like that. At least I hope not. She should be home by now."

Jessica took a deep breath. "Then what is it?"

"Mrs. Collins, Shelley has a drinking problem. Actually, I think we both do and it's getting worse. Cal's having an intervention for Shelley the first thing in the morning, and you should be there."

"Why didn't he call me?"

"I guess he didn't want Shelley to hear. He asked me to call you. Can you be there?"

"Of course, I will be there. What time?"

"Around nine."

"Thank you, Nance, for letting me know. What about you? Are you getting some help?"

"I think it may be too late for me, Mrs. Collins. Hopefully, it isn't too late for Shelley."

Jessica's head was spinning. She had a million questions but didn't know where to start. Since that episode in school when Shelley was twelve, she had never seen her daughter take more than a drink or two. How could this be happening?

"Nance, are you sure about this? It doesn't make sense."

"Just go in the morning. You will understand then."

"Okay, Nancy. Thank you again for calling me." They hung up.

There was no way Jessica could sleep now. She put on a pot of coffee and paced the floor wondering what she h ad done wrong. She thought of her divorce and remarriage. Both had been a huge mistake. Could that have caused this? She wasn't a psychologist, but was convinced this was her fault somehow. This couldn't be happening.

When Shelley married Cal, had Dani, and quit her job, Jessica worried that she would be restless. Cal was a great husband, but she had h er doubts about Shelley's feeling for him. Shelley had never wanted to be pinned down in a relationship. Cal let Shelley do whatever she wanted, and Jessica thought that was what might make it work. Shelley even spent a week skiing with friends when Deni was a baby, and Cal stayed home from work to care for her.

Shelley had seemed delighted with Dani, but often talked of her single days with a longing that worried Jessica. Yet in all that, Jessica never suspected alcohol to be an issue.

There must be a mistake. Nancy was wrong; that was all there was to it. She would get to the bottom of this.

Jessica jumped into the shower, dressed and began the two-hour drive to her daughter's house. It was only half past five, but this needed to be dealt with immediately. Jessica was convinced that there was some mistake. Perhaps it as just the argument between Shelley and her friend. They had been friends a long time, and even the best of friends have intense disagreements. Yes, that hat to be the answer. Nancy did sound strange. Perhaps she had been drinking herself. She did say that she had a problem with alcohol as well. Maybe she was confused.

> There is not so much comfort in having children as there is in sorry with parting with them.
>
> Proverb

A PARENT'S WORST NIGHTMARE

Jessica was surprised to find Dani up and watching cartoons so early. She said her mommy was outside smoking. Smoking? When did Shelley start smoking again?

At that moment, her daughter came in the back door, wearing her robe and slippers and looking like she had been in the middle of a tsunami.

"Mom? What are you doing here so early?"

"Nancy called. She said you were in some kind of trouble."

They both looked at Dani, who watched them with a worried expression.

Michelle motioned to the back door. "Maybe we should go outside."

Jessica kissed her granddaughter and followed Michelle out the door. "It will be all right," she assured Dani, who didn't look convinced.

"When did you start smoking? Jessica asked her daughter.

"I smoked when I was in high school. You know that."

"But I thought you quit."

"Sometimes I smoke when I feel stressed."

"Are you stressed now?"

"Things aren't going well between me and Cal, Mom."

"Nancy said you were drinking."

"She and I had a big fight this weekend. She's doing drugs and drinking, and gets paranoid. She threatened to call you. I got mad at her and broke the mirror on her car." Michelle started to cry. "Sometimes I don't know what I'm doing. Mom, I've been having blackouts." Michelle cried harder.

Jessica wrapped her arms around her daughter in complete confusion. "How long has this been going on? You seemed fine last time we were together."

"I'm just not good at this marriage thing, Mom. I can't seem to get through the day without a drink."

"I had no idea, Shelley, but it sounds like you might need to get some help." "I know, Mom. Cal told me he was having an intervention today, but I told him to forget it. I am going into rehab on Monday morning."

"Honey, that's great. Why don't I take Dani for the rest of the weekend so you and Cal can work things out?"

"Mom, there's nothing wrong with Cal. It's me. I just don't want to be here." Michelle continued crying for another five minutes.

Jessica shook her head, feeling completely helpless. She didn't have the first idea how to help her daughter. Rehab must be the answer. Everything would be okay after rehab.

> If everything seems under control, you're just not going fast enough.
> —Mario Andretti

REHAB

The first trip to rehab was terrifying. I didn't know what to expect or how I would survive. I didn't want to face myself, or remember what I had done. I just wanted to go to sleep and let it be over. My family and friends—those I still have left—believed I would return to my old self. They were so hopeful. Not me.

Detox was actually pretty easy, though. Mostly I just slept. They gave me IV fluids and Ativan to prevent the chance of seizures. It wasn't until many rehab stints later that I realized what the seizures were like. There was definitely a good reason for the Ativan.

They kept me on the Ativan for the first week, but then they began taking it away. That's when the anxiety started. Alcohol had become my best friend. How could I live without my friend?

By the second week, I began participating in the group discussions. A few of us started hanging out in the recreation room. We even got a band together, and I sang with them. It was like a party.

Most people don't realize it, but rehab for many becomes an escape from all the pressures of our lives. We needed to get away from all the guilt and judgment around us, people telling us how wrong we were, how much we were hurting them. They didn't understand us. Inside these walls, we all understood. Inside, it was okay to be us.

We all knew we would go back to our *friends* when we got out. Some even managed to sneak in a few pills to help us along. We didn't give each other a hard time or call each other out like they do in the movies. Hell, no! We all knew how it was. Going through the detox process allowed us to ease back into our addictions without the shakes and side effects, but we would go back. We all came back.

The second rehab was like a country club. It was on a river with beautiful grounds and gardens. People paid a fortune for their families to go there and had no idea what a good time they were having. During the day, there were classes on addictions. We passed each other notes and made jokes about the instructors. After a while, we all became experts; we knew more than most doctors.

At night, we hung out, told jokes, played music, laughed, and partied without the booze and pills. There was a lot of sex. The counselors had no idea, but a lot of people used sex to cope with the absence of their preferred substance.

Counseling sessions involved family members and one-on-one therapy. There were many events, things, and people we could blame for our addictions. My major complaint was boredom. I was bored, and when I was bored, I drank. Or I was stressed, and when I was stressed, I drank. I also drank when I was happy.

One counselor nailed me when he said that there would always be reasons for drinking. The only time I would stop was when I wanted to be sober more than I wanted to be drunk. I tried to ignore that. It was much easier to blame my husband, my daughter, my mom, and my life in general. The truth was I just liked to drink.

After a while, I wanted to avoid facing the things I had done and said when I was drunk. I forgot a lot of them, but I could still remember enough that it made me want to burrow into that vodka bottle again and again.

As the rehabs became more frequent, they also became less luxurious. Money was getting tighter and tighter and family members were getting less and less supportive. They all expected the first rehab to change me. Then they blamed the rehab and thought a better one would do the job. None of them seemed to understand that the only one who could change me was me, and I wasn't ready yet.

> To love one's self is the beginning of a lifelong romance.
> —Oscar Wilde

I STILL WANT MY MOMMY BACK

Dani came home from school each day with one question. Was Mommy sick? After she went to the "hab" place, she seemed okay for a while. The "hab" place was supposed to make her better, but it never seemed to last very long.

Dani went to a meeting at one of the places where she sat with other kids and talked about how they felt. The only thing she could say was that she wanted the old Mommy back. This new Mommy scared her.

Dani told them it was her fault that her mommy was sick, and that she kept trying to be good so Mommy would get well. The worst thing was that she thought the old Mommy might never come back.

Some days when she came home from school, Mommy wasn't home at all. She was probably at the place where they all drank from dark bottles and laughed a lot. When she went there, she came home happy; but then she would go to sleep right away, leaving Dani to watch cartoons until Dad came home and made her dinner.

The bad day Dani will always remember. It was the worst day of all. Dani had just gotten off the bus when she saw Mommy putting a suitcase in her car. "Where are you going, Mommy? Am I going with you? Is Dad going with us?"

Mommy was crying, and she looked bad again. It had been three weeks since the last "hab", and Dani was hoping she was getting better.

"I'm sorry, baby. I just can't do this anymore. Daddy will be home soon. I just called him."

"When will you be back, Mommy?"

"I don't know, Dani. I just have to go now."

Her mother got in the car and began to drive away when Dani realized she might never see her mommy again. Dani began running after the car. "Stop, Mommy, take me with you. Don't leave me. Stop!"

The car slowed briefly, and Dani though her mother might be returning, but then it sped up again and disappeared around the corner. Dani sat on the ground at the end of the driveway sobbing. That was where her dad found her when he got home an hour later.

> Your children will see what you're all about by what you live rather than what you say.
>
> —Wayne Dyer

HALFWAY HOUSE TO HELL

While the rehabs were a respite, the halfway houses were pure hell. Following the first rehab, we all expected—surprisingly, even me—that the worst was over. I was now cured and would go back to my life.

I sat down and told Dani to always ask to sip my large drink of juice or soda. If she ever saw me drinking anything else, I told her, she should take it away from me. What a joke! That lasted exactly eight days. I quickly stopped allowing my daughter to sip my drinks as they now contained large quantities of vodka.

Now that the cat was out of the bag and I no longer needed to attempt to appear normal, my drinking became nonstop. I began in the morning and continued throughout the night. There seemed no reason to stop. Everyone knew I was a drunk, so who cared?

After I put Dani to bed—or more often she put herself to bed—I would pass out on the sofa. Sometime after that, I would waken and wander about in search for more liquor. Often, I even left the house and drove to an all-night liquor store. The next day, I would find the car on the next block in the middle of the street. Frequently, there would be dents and scrapes on the car, but I couldn't remember how or when I got them.

Cal had long since given up trying to get me to stay in bed or looking for me at night. He tried taking sleeping pills so that he wouldn't hear me clomping around, but he was afraid Dani might need him, or I would do something radical.

Twice I had to be taken to the emergency room for hurting myself. Once I almost lost an eye because I fell against a lamp. At best, I usually woke with bumps and bruises from falling or hitting something. I could never remember how it happened.

Consequently, following my second time in rehab, I was told I would enter a halfway house. The neighborhoods with large leafy trees and neatly trimmed yards had no desire for a house filled with drunks and addicts near their beautiful, pristine homes and healthy families.

The halfway houses, therefore, were usually in the middle of some of the worst neighborhoods, surrounded by bars and drug dealers. They had to be on a bus route because we were expected to work.

Since most of us had lost our careers due to our addictions, the only jobs we could get paid minimum wage. We had to pass through the bar laden streets to get to the bus stops and go to work at jobs we hated. None of us handled stress well and resented being told what to do. This was not the life we wanted. Most of us didn't last long before we just went into the nearest bar and forgot about work.

Some of the counselors were recovering addicts, and several times, they relapsed and brought drugs into the houses themselves. Fights often broke out over the drugs, and occasionally, boyfriends appeared to muddy the waters even more. The boyfriends often brought even more drugs and precipitated even more fights, often violent ones.

One girl, whose boyfriend came to the house to break up with her, took a bunch of pills and completely wigged out. She broke a window on the third floor and tried to jump out of it. They had to take her back to detox.

These events seemed to justify falling of the wagon. After all, it wasn't my fault that I was surrounded by all this turmoil. I needed a drink.

There are some experiences that I remember vividly and wish with all my being that I could forget. One such time was when I took Dani to church. She was allowed to visit me for a few hours on Sunday. Cal would pick her up in the evening.

I wanted to take her to church. I was still hanging on to my faith, hoping that God would not give up on me. After the service, I decided we should have lunch and watch a sports event that I had been following. Naturally, the restaurant I chose served liquor. I would just have a beer with lunch. Beer doesn't count. Right?

After a few beers, we wandered back to the halfway house. Dani was very quiet and seemed to be near tears. I couldn't understand what her problem was. The halfway house recognized that I had been drinking and was ready to kick me out. Dani was now crying openly. They couldn't reach Cal, and by the time he picked her up, she was hysterical. After that, she never trusted me again.

I went through several halfway houses. The story was usually the same. Once someone relapsed, the whole house followed suit. Some made it through their six months, but I never got past a few weeks.

I made one good friend. She and I bonded on day one. We were about the same age and both loved music. She survived her six months and went home. We vowed to stay in touch and get together regularly. I never saw her again. I heard she relapsed and went back to rehab.

> Learning to trust is one of life's most difficult tasks.
> —Isaac Watts

LOSING HOPE

Michelle had just returned from her latest rehab stint and had been on Antabuse for a while. Cal began to think his prayers had finally been answered and that she was going to be okay. It took only a few weeks before his hope began to deteriorate into complete despair. Cal knew Michelle had relapsed when he saw the bright red blotches on her face and neck. Then he found the Antabuse tablets in the trash. It was beginning again.

Most evenings when he returned from work, he would find Dani watching television and eating cereal from a box while Shelley slept on the couch. Things were okay while she was asleep. He would cook dinner for Dani, and they would eat in the kitchen. They would talk about school and her friends, trying to ignore the passed-out, drunken mother on the sofa.

Sometimes Shelley never even made it to the sofa. Cal might find her completely passed out in the car, with the engine still running, door open. Cal knew he was going to have to hide the car keys, but dreaded his wife's tirade when he did so.

It was when Shelley woke up that the problems began. She would stumble around trying to make another drink. She was always cranky when she first woke, cursing at him and Dani for some imagined misdeed. He would try to get her to eat something, but she never wanted to eat; the food interfered with the effect of the vodka.

The rest of the evening was a nightmare. She would drink until she passed out again, but then wake up in the middle of the night screaming at him.

"I hate you," she would yell. "You have ruined my life. I should never have married you. I should never have had Dani."

While Cal desperately wanted to care for his daughter, he was struggling to focus on anything but the pain. He kept asking himself *why?* He went to work every day, fearing he would lose his job if he didn't, but not wanting to speak to anyone or caring about anything. Except for the pain, the only thing he felt was empty.

The bills were piling up. Some, he just forgot to pay; but the medical bills were astronomical, and he kept buying Dani presents she didn't need just to make her happy. He began maxing out his credit cards. His boss was trying to be understanding about the situation, but Cal had missed a lot of work trying to cope with his depression, care for Dani, and go to the legal and medical appointments necessary to make things normal again.

When he did have time off, he knew he should pick up the house, do the laundry, dishes, and so on. The house was beginning to look like a pigsty He had never realized just how much Shelley had taken care of things, at least in the beginning. However, he could never seem to find the energy to do more than absolutely necessary.

He kept telling himself that Michelle was sick. She needed help. It really wasn't his Shelly who said those things. She would get better. He went to group sessions at the treatment facilities and Al-Anon meetings. They all said the same thing. He could not enable her. He had to protect his daughter.

Finally, the day Cal came home and found Dani sobbing hysterically at the end of the driveway, he realized that he had to do something. It took him over an hour to calm his daughter down enough to tell him what happened. The next morning, he called an attorney and filed for custody.

> Black holes are where God divided by zero
> —Steven Wright

A PARENT'S GUILT

Jessica was beside herself with fear and worry. She worried about Dani. Was Dani safe? Was she scared? What should she do? She tried to take Dani for the weekend whenever possible, but Dani was in school and seemed terrified to leave her father for more than a day.

She called Shelley every day. After each rehab, she prayed that this one would be the one that finally worked. She would have her daughter back.

When Shelley answered the phone, there was that split second when Jessica would hold her breath, waiting for that telltale sound in her daughter's voice. Was she drinking again? Shelley could be warm and loving, until she took that first drink. Then, there was that edge to her voice. She would become angry and blaming. Shelley blamed Jessica, she blamed Cal, and she even blamed Dani for being born.

After numerous conversations with Cal—Jessica had developed the highest respect for him—they decided that Dani could not be left alone with Michelle. She often took Dani with her in the car. She'd had several minor accidents. Fortunately, no one had been hurt. Yet.

The problem was that Shelley would fly into a rage when the sitter arrived. She could easily manipulate the young ones but only succeeded in making the older ones, who refused to listen to her, quit after a few days.

Jessica and Cal both realized that, for Dani's sake, Cal would have to file for custody and ask Shelley to leave the house. Jessica agonized over her conflicting loyalties to her daughter and granddaughter. What would happen to Shelley if she left the relative safety of her home with Cal?

Knowing that Shelley might have to leave, Jessica pleaded with her daughter to come and stay with her.

"Come home, Shell. It will be okay. I will go to AA meetings with you. We will get through this together. I love you."

Michelle could hear in her mother's voice that she was saying *You can't drink*. She knew without question that the one boundary that her mother would impose was a total ban on alcohol.

"Mom, you know that won't work. We would never get along."

Jessica knew that was Shelley's way of saying she could not be without her alcohol.

When Shelley left her home for the last time, Jessica had a terrible time locating her. She never answered her phone, and Jessica had no idea where her daughter was. When Shelley finally called her, she said she dropped her phone in the trash and had to buy one from a convenience store. She didn't have many minutes, though, so they couldn't talk often.

Jessica could tell that her daughter was very drunk. She wouldn't say where she was living, and Jessica was terrified for her.

The nights were long. Jessica tossed and turned with visions of her daughter in a ditch or being abducted or... She was losing weight and was having a hard time concentrating on her work. Like Cal, she feared she would lose her job, but she couldn't conjure up the energy or interest to care. She just wanted her daughter to be healthy again.

During one of their conversations, Shelley admitted that she had tried to stop drinking and was staying with some friends who had taken her in. She agreed to go to the emergency room if she couldn't stop on her own. Jessica had doubts, but she prayed Shelley would do as she promised.

> Obstacles are those frightful things you
> see when you take your eyes off your goal.
> —Henry Ford

SATURDAY NIGHT AT THE EMERGENCY ROOM

It was Saturday night at the emergency room. Who knew this was the place to be for us drunks and addicts. What a party! This was my third trip to the ER. I usually went straight from the ER to detox to rehab. The first time in the emergency room, I toughed it out without my bottle, but I learned fast. We all knew we would be here for hours. The chairs had filled up early, and people lounged on the floor against the wall, passing plastic bags of pills and containers filled with vodka. We shared. We were good people.

A few stared, glassy eyed, at the floor, some shaking uncontrollably, until someone gave them a hit of something that would take the edge off. Mostly we joked and laughed. This was our purgatory. Someone giggled. We all knew that once we passed those doors into the treatment rooms, they would take away our stash, so we used as much as we could.

After a while, some began to trickle out. F this, they would say, and just stagger out the door. No one tried to stop them. Some had family members and friends with them, but most were just dumped off, kind of like the weekly garbage to be disposed of somehow. The security cameras were working, but the security staff mostly ignored us unless someone got too loud.

As the hours wore on, some of those who were there for injuries and illnesses would complain about the wait. One mother asked if her son could be given something for pain.

"We can't dispense drugs until we get into the treatment room. Too many addicts just come here to score, then leave. I know we're backed up, but on Saturday, the drunks all seem to come out of the woodwork. They'll probably mostly disappear before they get to treatment, but for now, we are overloaded."

The woman looked around at those of us who were tagged as "the drunks and addicts." The look of disgust was familiar. *Why are they clogging up the emergency room?* We were just scum, she was thinking.

Sometime after midnight, they took me into a room with a cot. As I knew they would, they took away my bottle and the pills I had in my bag. It didn't take long before the shaking started, but the Ativan they gave me calmed me down right away. They hooked me up to an IV, and I fell asleep.

The dark night was fading to gray when they woke me and told me that my insurance didn't cover detox at this hospital. They were letting me go. They gave me a list of detox and rehab facilities. I had already been to most of them. I threw the list in the trash.

As I walked out into the city street, I looked for a clock to decide if the liquor stores were open yet. I spotted a park across the street from a sign that advertised liquor. A few people were sitting on benches and waiting for the store to open. I recognized some of them from the ER. I sat down with them, and waited.

Hate the disease, not the diseased.
—Anonymous

YOU AND ME AGAINST THE WORLD

After Shelley left for the final time, Dani and Cal seemed to have formed an unspoken agreement not to mention her. They sat together on the sofa watching movies that neither of them really saw. They ate meals together that they seldom finished. Dani was never more than two feet away from Cal when he was home. She would greet him as he walked in the door from work with that haunting look as though she had some deep secret pain, a pain that he shared. They bonded together in their pain.

Sometimes Dani would panic if she couldn't find him, shrieking in terror. He tried to stay close to her, but there were times when he would escape to the basement to play music and avoid the hurt for a short time. Or he would turn on the shower and sob, hoping his daughter couldn't hear him.

After Dani went to bed, he would search the house for Shelley's stashed vodka bottles and throw them in the trash. One night, however, he decided to pour himself a drink from one of the bottles. The alcohol seemed to ease the pain somewhat, so he put the bottle in the cabinet. The nightly drink, or two, quickly became a habit and he actually bought a bottle for himself.

Dani had a nightmare one night and came running down the stairs to find him as he was finishing his second drink of the night. When she saw the drink, she curled into a ball and cried so hard she began to hiccup.

"You will go away too. Just like Mommy," she sobbed between hiccups.

Cal held her close and promised her he would never leave her like that. He walked to the sink and poured out the remainder of the drink. Then he tossed the bottle into the trash. No more drinking for him after that.

The next morning, he almost tripped over Dani as he was leaving his bedroom. She had taken her sleeping bag and put it outside his door. Try as he might, he could not convince her to sleep in her bed. She would get into her bed each night, but as soon as he was asleep, she would move her bag outside his door and sleep there for the remainder of the night. Her eyes developed the dark circles of someone who has not had enough sleep.

Dani continued to look at him with a question in her eyes. Would he leave her like her mommy had? She stopped laughing entirely, and seldom talked. They ate in silence, and she refused to go anywhere without him.

They obviously needed counseling, so he made an appointment for them together. At first, Dani refused to talk at all; but after a while, she shared her worry that he would leave and she would be alone. She missed her mommy but was afraid of her at the same time. Her grades were barely passing, and she often made excuses for staying home from school.

Cal's work suffered from missed time to care for Dani, and he feared he would lose his income. He hired a woman to stay with Dani after school while he was at work, but

Dani didn't like her and would stay in her room until Cal came home.

The tension was causing him all kinds of medical issues, back problems, high blood pressure. Cal started taking an antidepressant, which helped a little, and he continued talking to the counselor, sometimes with Dani and sometimes alone.

Eventually, the pain eased, but never disappeared entirely. He put away all the old pictures of their happy times together and tried to live his life.

> Just because you have a nightmare, doesn't mean you have to stop dreaming.
> —Jill Scott

ANTABUSE—THE LAST RESORT

After the last rehab, I tried Antabuse. I actually asked for it. They didn't want to give it to me but then eventually gave in. They said if I drank while taking it, I could die. It was either abstinence or the morgue, my counselor said.

For a while, it did work. I believed that I had no choice. I took the pill every morning, telling myself that for today, I could not drink. It didn't do much for the stress, however, and I was on edge, constantly wanting a drink. A lot of people in rehab recommended those high-energy drinks with tons of caffeine. It was like a different kind of high.

I usually picked them up at the local Wawa, but one evening, I decided to pick one up at the liquor store, which was closer to my house. I guess you might call that a subconscious form of sabotage, because I had to know that it would have alcohol in it.

The first sip tasted so much better than my usual high-energy stuff. After three or four gulps, I realized my mistake, but I finished the can right there in the car. I could feel the flush almost immediately. I raced home and looked in the mirror. My eyes looked like something from *Village of the Damned*. My heart was racing, and my face was beet red. I was sure I would die. Perhaps it was for the best; it would put all of us out of our misery.

Unfortunately, I lived. Cal came home and suggested I take Xanax. That seemed to help. The next morning, I didn't take the Antabuse.

> To many, total abstinence is easier than perfect moderation.
> —St. Augustine

HITTING BOTTOM

I got myself in a box and didn't know how to get out. The last few months had been complete hell. After I stopped taking the Antabuse, I went back into rehab and then to another halfway house. I got kicked out of that one after two weeks when I got caught drinking cough syrup. Crap, I didn't think they would figure that one out.

I knew Cal was finished with me and that I couldn't go home this time. He had filed papers with an attorney so that I couldn't see Dani without supervision, and I could not spend the night at home. My options were getting fewer and fewer.

Leaving my luggage behind, I threw what I could into a tote bag and walked out. This halfway house was in one of the worst parts of the city. There were bars on every block, and I started hitting them, one by one.

That first night was a blur. I went home with some woman who stole my cell phone (my money was in my sock, so she couldn't find it). I think she must have beaten me up because I woke up with bruises on my face and arms. She was out, so I used her shower and left before she returned.

Surprisingly, I still had my looks. I had lost about twenty pounds, but with a little makeup over the bruises, I still looked good enough to get guys to buy me drinks. Some of those guys weren't so nice when I wouldn't go home with them. One in particular started cussing me out and dragging me toward the door.

There were a few people shooting pool at one end of the bar, and they yelled at him to let go of me. I thanked them and then proceed to pass out right in front of them. They took me home that night and told me I could stay until I found another place. It turned out they were all related and lived in the same house.

For some reason, they seemed to like me. Go figure. I doubted that there was much left to like. My options were getting pretty slim. I knew if I called my mother or Cal, they would put me in detox again, and I wasn't ready for another detox.

I was getting really scared. Somewhere in my foggy brain, I realized that I would die if I didn't stop drinking. It turned out that the people who took me in were actually AA members who had been in recovery for years. I didn't bother to notice that they were drinking Cokes when I met them. The only came to shoot pool. I hated pool, but any port in the storm. It was better than the alley where I was likely to end up next.

It took only a few days before they began their campaign to get me into recovery. Sure, I knew I needed to stop drinking, get my life back. It didn't take a brain surgeon to figure that out. But I was terrified of being without my crutch. Looking at my like, facing that I had done without that numbing blur was just too scary. It turned out it was even tougher than I expected.

My body refused to let go of the alcohol. I would try not drinking for an hour, sometimes two, but then the shakes would start, along with the pain, as if my whole being was screaming for a drink.

I knew I could go into detox and they would give me something to get me down, but then I would have to go through the rehab-and-halfway-house thing again. I couldn't face that. For one thing, I was out of insurance and money. That was no option. I needed to go this one alone.

Each night I fell asleep—or pass out—with the intention that tomorrow would be the end. I would not take another drink. Usually, I didn't make it to morning before the craving woke me, and I would stumble around until I found my latest stash of vodka.

I had to hide it from my new friends because they would take it away from me. They kept asking me to go to a meeting, but that too was scary. There had been AA meetings in rehab. They were okay because I was always sober in rehab. How could I go to AA in my condition? I felt like such a failure!

Finally, I was able to make it through two days without a drink. It was a miracle—or so I thought. I woke up on the bathroom floor, my head was bleeding, and I must have knocked over a glass. Fortunately, someone heard then noise and found me.

They said I'd had a seizure. This is common reaction to severe withdrawal from alcohol. They said I needed Ativan or Valium to get through it. The problem was that I couldn't get it from my doctor without going back into detox, and I was too afraid to have another seizure. I was in a box.

I have not failed. I've just found 10,000 ways that won't work.
—Thomas Alva Edison

ALCOHOLICS ANONYMOUS

It took me three tries to actually make it inside the room. The first two times, I stood outside and watched as groups formed tight circles, smoking, and drinking coffee. There was also a lot of pastry being passed around. I guess the drugs of choice in recovery are caffeine, nicotine, and sugar.

The people seemed friendly; some smiled at me and said hello. But I felt like a fraud since I was far from sober both times. The third try, one of my housemates walked with me into the room and assured me that not every person who entered was sober.

Looking around, I realized she was telling the truth. Some were clearly drunk or high. Many fidgeted, with their legs shaking up and down, or tapping their fingers or toes. Some were dozing.

The significant factor, however, was that none were judged. Drunk or sober, everyone was welcome. The only rule was that you couldn't use while in the meeting or bring in contraband. Some clearly violated that last rule.

I was convinced that this wasn't for me. God had forsaken me a long, long time ago, I was certain. I waited, listening to all the testimony, eager to leave. I had tried, right? That was all I could do. I didn't need to go back.

As we walked from the meeting, a woman about ten years my senior approached me. She wasn't actually smiling, but she seemed friendly. She was definitely heading in my direction. What could she possibly want with me?

I tried to ease out the door before she could reach me, but I was too late. She was already extending her hand and smiling. I was trapped.

"I've seen you outside during the past few meetings. Happy to see you made it in this time."

I opened my mouth to explain how this just wasn't for me, but she continued,

"The first time is rough. The God thing gets to some people in the beginning. But the important thing is that you are here. This is the beginning of your recovery."

She obviously didn't realize that I'd consumed a good bit of vodka before coming here in order to avoid the inevitable shakes during the two-hour abstinence.

She shook her head as though reading my mind. "I had a few before I came to my first meeting. Give it a chance. It will get better."

I nodded my thanks politely and turned to leave once again.

"If you will let me, I would like to be your sponsor." Seeing my look of horror, she continued, "Don't worry, I won't drag you to church or meetings, but if it's okay, I would like to call now and then and have coffee together."

I mutely handed over my phone number and then stumbled out the door. A sponsor? I didn't want or need a sponsor; I just needed a drink. I could feel her eyes on me, so I quickly walked away from the church hall.

He who has a why to live, can bear with almost any how.
—Friedrich Nietzsche

FREEDOM

The moment I opened my eyes, I knew something was different. Walking into the bathroom, I examined my eyes, washed my mouth out, and brushed my teeth. My eyes were clear; my mouth didn't taste like a layer of stale cat fur. My stomach didn't lurch threateningly. What was different?

Looking down at my hands, I realized that they weren't shaking. Something was definitely missing from my usual miserable morning.

That was it—the craving was gone! I was *free*. I had not felt this absence of intense craving for alcohol in years; I forgot how many. It was exhilarating.

I'd finally found a doctor who gave me a prescription for Ativan. I knew it wasn't ideal to do this on my own, but I just couldn't face another round of rehab.

Somehow I got through that dreaded three days without a seizure. I went to every AA meeting within a five-mile area. I tried eating, but I couldn't seem to keep anything down except doughnuts and coffee—and of course, my cigarettes. Now I know why the coffeepot is so huge at the meetings.

Each morning, when I woke, I rushed to the calendar to mark off another day without alcohol, and I would tell myself to just make it through one more. Each morning, my body screamed for another drink, just one more.

This morning, however, was different. Oh, I wanted a drink all right, but the significant thing was that I didn't have that craving, that feeling like one more minute without alcohol and my body would self-destruct. I couldn't believe it, but I was actually free.

I rushed to the phone to call my sponsor. Strangely, she didn't sound surprised, just happy. Was I cured?

"There is no cure, Shelley, just sobriety. This is the easy part. We start the hard part next. See you at the meeting."

Meeting? Why did I still need the meetings? I was cured, right?

Somehow, I trusted my sponsor and went to the meeting after all. That was when she started talking in earnest about the steps. Each meeting went over the steps, but I never really got beyond step one. I admitted that I was powerless. Okay, it took a while to accept that one. I never really addressed the others.

> To love oneself is the beginning of a lifelong romance.
> —Oscar Wilde

RECOVERY

There is no magic to the process of recovery. It is long and agonizing. There are occasional slips when a drink is the only way to survive the memories. Unfortunately, many of the memories returned, and with them the painful infusion of guilt and sorrow.

I knew I had ruined Dani's life. She looked at me with wariness, even now It took a long time before she would let me hug her again, and even longer before she would go somewhere with me in the car. We were taking small steps, and I prayed that I would get her trust back someday.

Cal would never forgive me; I had accepted that. I was trying to make amends, the ninth step, but my biggest mistake was in marrying him in the first place. I took advantage of his love, abused it, and finally used it up entirely.

I knew I had put my mom through hell, but she was just so ecstatic that I was sober again. She kept telling me that making amends was keeping sober and getting my life back. She kept sending me vitamins and pressuring me to quit smoking and to eat protein. She had done some research on recovery from alcoholism and said that a high-protein, low-carb diet was important, along with vitamins and minerals—and not smoking. Yikes!

She was probably right about a lot of it because I knew my brain was still foggy; I couldn't remember things or react to things the way I thought I should. I took the vitamins, but sugar, caffeine, and nicotine continued to be my survival foods.

What good would it do to struggle through these steps? Why was my sponsor pushing them so hard? They just seemed to hurt. Each one was more painful than the other. Okay, so step 1: yes, I knew I was powerless over my alcohol addiction. What good would it do to say it? Slowly I realized that I had never accepted the fact that I could not drink. It seemed so unfair.

My sponsor was patient with me; she never judged or argued, just kept telling me to take one step at a time. She reiterated the message that one of my counselors told me, that I would stop drinking when I wanted to be sober more than I wanted to be drunk, and I think at last that I did.

I never wanted to go back in that box; the very thought of it brought on a feeling of panic and suffocation. Remembering that feeling kept me from taking a drink during the long hours when I felt that I couldn't survive without my old "friend."

Steps 2 and 3, believing in a higher power, was easier. On my first day of freedom, I felt that God had returned to me. A daily visit to church to thank him became a vital part of my life. It was as though a healing spirit had entered my soul. I wished that I could convey that feeling to those who were rejecting the higher power.

Steps 4 and 5 slammed me in the face like a mule kick. I actually relapsed for an entire day trying to face the moral inventory of myself and admitting the nature of my wrongs.

Looking at the person I had become, I felt nauseous. It took weeks of struggle to finally move beyond that one.

Steps 6 and 7 I entered into greedily. Yes, I wanted God to remove my defects and eagerly asked for his forgiveness. These were the steps that enabled me to move beyond 4 and 5.

Steps 8 and 9 will continue to haunt me forever as I desperately try to make amends. As my memory returns, I also pile on more to the list of persons I had harmed during my drinking. Thanks to my new relationship with God, however, I realize that the person I harmed most was myself.

Steps 10 and 11 are an ongoing lifestyle. I find myself questioning each motive and action. Living right takes conscious thought, and I ask for God's help with every step.

I have yet to have the courage and confidence to begin step 12, but I hope that my growing strength will allow me to do so in the near future.

> To sit alone with my conscience will be judgment enough for me.
> —Charles William Stubbs

COMING FULL CIRCLE

I saw her enter the door with great trepidation. She looked around warily, before casting her eyes down and moving to a chair near the door. She had that closed-off look, as though she knew this could never work, yet at the same time praying that it would. She was in hell, and nothing was going to save her. It was like looking into a mirror five years earlier.

I could tell she was far from sober. Although young, probably in her twenties, she had aged with the ravages of the alcohol. The unsteady gait caused her to fumble clumsily for her chair. Her eyes were red and glassy. Her hair was uncombed and greasy, and her nails were frayed on the ends.

The most important thing, though, was that she was here. She had taken that first huge step. She didn't know it, but this would be the beginning of her recovery.

I grabbed two cups of coffee and a couple of doughnuts and sat down beside the young woman. She seemed startled by my presence, and I thought she might leave.

"These doughnuts aren't completely stale," I said, laughing. "The coffee is good and strong, though. It might help get you through the hour without a drink."

She looked up, surprised by my insight. "How did you know?"

"Oh, believe me, we have all been there." I looked around. "Many of us still are."

Handing her the coffee, I quickly introduced myself. "Hi, I'm Shelley, and if you let me, I would like to be your sponsor."

> In the end, we will remember not the words of our enemies, but the silence of our friends.
> —Martin Luther King, Jr.

AUTHOR'S NOTE

There are numerous theories regarding the causes of alcoholism. The Adverse Childhood Experience (ACE) Questionnaire identifies an individual's level of childhood trauma. It is suggested that traumatic events during childhood may increase one's chances of alcoholism and other addictions.

Trauma is not always easily identified. The character in the book you just completed did not suffer abuse or overt neglect. However, she had numerous experiences that left her feeling disconnected. The feeling, which has often been described as anomie by sociologists and psychologists, is often the source of depression and anxiety.

We respond to life experiences in various ways. It is important to identify areas of need and to maintain a social and spiritual support network to prevent that feeling of disconnect.

What is the answer to this problem? For those who fear they may be at risk, *get help now!*

If you care about someone and you believe they are at risk, *do not passively watch*. Most importantly, do not contribute to the problem. Be part of the solution, not the problem. Don't drink with them. Don't encourage their drinking. Instead, provide resources for help.

Create a safe haven for children, giving them a healthy structure as much as possible. One solid relationship with a responsible adult can make the difference in their future response to the ongoing trauma. Do not involve them in the crises that often occur, but help them to trust that there is a support network for them.

Children frequently believe they are to blame for the problems created by alcohol. Do not allow them to feel responsible, or feel that they have the Power to change the alcoholic's behavior.

In addition to AA, local emergency rooms will provide information about detox and rehabilitation facilities even if they do not offer the services themselves. Talk to them. Become informed. Go to an Al-Anon meeting. Most of all, *don't let them drive drunk!*

Alcoholics Anonymous has helped many people recover their lives. Many resist and are concerned about the religious emphasis, feeling that they have been abandoned by God. Yet those who accept God's love often increase their chances of recovery. Many feel completely alone and disconnected. Recognizing that they are not alone aids in the healing process significantly.

Yet AA does not force members to accept the higher power; it merely makes them aware of the concept of unconditional love. Those who choose not to actively participate may just listen. They are encouraged to take it a step at a time and to use the Serenity Prayer as a guide.

The Serenity Prayer had been adopted by all twelve step groups, and the first few lines are used during the meetings. It has been attributed to St. Francis d Assisi. However, the prayer was written in the 1930s by Reinhold Niebuhr. The prayer is as follows:

> *God, give me grace to accept with serenity*
> *the things that cannot be changed,*
> *Courage to change the things*
> *which should be changed,*
> *and the Wisdom to distinguish*
> *the one from the other.*
> *Living one day at a time,*
> *Enjoying one moment at a time,*
> *Accepting hardships as a pathway to peace,*
> *Taking, as Jesus did,*
> *This sinful world as it is,*
> *Not as I would have it,*
> *Trusting that You will make all things right,*
> *If I surrender to Your will,*
> *So that I may be reasonably happy in this life,*
> *And supremely happy with You forever in the next.*
> *Amen.*

The first part of the prayer can be a guide by which all of us can live. Look at your obstacles and identify which ones you can change and which ones you cannot. If you have the ability to change your situation, do so. If you do not, let it go. Try not to do everything at once, but take daily steps toward the person you would like to become.

ALCOHOLICS ANONYMOUS
A.A. World Services, Inc.,
P.O. Box 459,
Grand Central Station
New York, NY 10163
(212)870-3400

The best way out is always through
—Robert Frost

BIBLIOGRAPHY

Alcoholics Anonymous World Service, Inc. (2001). *The Big Book of AA, 4th Edition*.

Alexander, Walter (1996). *Drug Topics, Vol. 140*, No. 4, Feb 19, pp. 56-58.

American Psychiatric Association. (1994). *Diagnostic and Statistical Manual of Mental Disorders, IV-It Edition*. Washington, D.C.

Bailey, K.P. The brain's rewarding system & addiction. *Journal of Psychosocial Nursing* 2004:42(6): 14-18.

Frankl, Viktor E. (1959) *Man's Search for Meaning*. New York: Simon & Schuster, Inc.

Giordano, John J. (2006). *Proven holistic treatment for addiction & chronic relapse*. Mustang, Oklahoma: Tate Publishing.

Hart, Peter D. and Teeter, Robert M. (2004). *Addiction Carries Huge Stigma and Shame*. Survey Report by Hart Research and Coldwater Corporation.

Knapp, Caroline. (1996). *Drinking: A love story*. New York Bantam Dell

LeDoux, J. E. (1996). *The emotional brain: the mysterious underpinnings of emotional life*. New York: Simon & Shuster.

Milam, James R & Ketcham, Katherine. (1983). *Under the Influence: A guide to the myths and realities of alcoholism*. New York: Bantam Books.

Miller, Wm. R. & Rollnick, S. (1991). *Motivational Interviewing: Preparing People to Change Addictive Behavior*. New York: Guildford Press.

Mills, C.W. (1959). *The sociological imagination*. London: Oxford.

Nathan, P.E. The role of natural recovery in alcoholism and pathological gambling. *Journal of gambling Studies*, 2003; .19 (3), 279-286.

Nester, Eric J and Malenka, Robert C. The Addicted Brain. *Scientific American, March* 2004: 78-85.

Prentiss, Chris. The Alcoholism and Addiction Cure: A holistic approach to total recovery. (2007. Power Press: Los Angeles, CA.

Prochaska, J. O., & DiClemente, C. C. (1986). Toward a comprehensive model of change. In W. R. Miller & N. Heather (Eds.) *Treating Addictive Behaviors: Processes of Change*, (pp. 3-27). New York: Plenum Press.

Pulay, A. J. Dawson, D. A., Hasin, D. S., Goldstein, R. B., Ruan, W. J., Pickering, R. P., Huang, B., Chou, S. P., Grant, B. F. (December 12, 2007). Violent Behavior and DSM-IV Psychiatric Disorders: Results from the National Epidemiologic Survey on Alcohol and Related Conditions. *Journal of Clinical Psychiatry*.

Rimland, Bernard (2008). *Dyslogic Syndrome*. Kingsley Publishers.

Seligman, M.E.P. (1974). Depression and Learned Helplessness. In R. J. Friedman & M. M. Katz (Eds), *The psychology of depression: Contemporary theory and research*. New York: Wiley.

Seligman, M.E.P. (1991). Learned optimism. New York Knopf.

Sun Tzu (1988). Thomas Cleary (Trans.). *The Art of War*. Boston: Shambhala.

Walls, Jeannette. (2005). *The Glass Castle*. New York: Scribner.

Printed in the USA
CPSIA information can be obtained
at www.ICGtesting.com
CBHW071311200724
11858CB00023B/580